CHANAKYA NEETI

For Students
In English

PRIYANKA GULSHAN

MW01537723

Acknowledgement

In this book, an attempt has been made to translate
the words of Acharya Chanakya into simple words.
Any line or sentence used in this book is a verse
spoken by Acharya Chanakya which is explained
in simple language. And all those lines are being
used appropriately to educate the students and to
promote knowledge related to the history of our
own country INDIA .
I have only done translations in this book and
therefore cannot take the full credit for this book.
Rather The entire credit of this book goes
to Acharya Chanakya.
Because his words have guided all of us till today
and will also guide us in future too .

Copyright © Priyanka Gulshan 2020

A disciple pays tribute to
Acharya Chanakya

Tvam-Eva Maataa
-Cha Pitaa Tvam-Eva

Tvam-Eva Bandhush
-Cha Sakhaa Tvam-Eva

Tvam-Eva Viidyaa
Dravinnam Tvam-Eva

Tvam-Eva Sarvam
Mama Deva Deva

Meaning -

You Truly are my Mother And You
Truly are my Father .
You Truly are my Relative And You
Truly are my Friend.
You Truly are my Knowledge and You
Truly are my Wealth.
You Truly are my All, My God of Gods.

INDEX

#1

Acharya Chanakya said that -

" The ideal king is one whose
Body, mind and soul all three are strong,
Why all three ?
If the king is weak from his body
he will not be able to handle his army,
And if he is weak
And has an unstable mind,
he will be defeated
With his own concerns.
And if his soul is weak
Then how will he give strength
to his people ? "

Meaning -
Acharya Chanakya gave us an example of a
king and explained how a king should be firm
with his body, mind and soul, in the same way
a student should also be strong with his body,
mind and soul because if a student is
weakened by his body, then he will only get
entangled in the web of diseases and will
never be able to focus on his goal.
And if his mind becomes weak and unstable,
that is, if he is not able to keep his mind under
control, then surely his attention will continue
to wander.

" The Bhagawat Gita also mentions the mind
{ Mann } being like an unbridled horse. "
And the importance has been given to the
way in which a person should keep his mind
under his control,
Otherwise this unbridled horse can also take
him to the ditch.
And a student must also be strong from his
spirit.
But how can one be strong with his soul ?
Yes, the soul is {Ajay} undefeatable,
immortal {Amar} and invisible as well !
But the word soul has been used here to
signify that we have to become so strong from
within ourselves, that whatever we are
determined to do, we will be able to achieve it
with our hard-work and concentration.
It should not be our objective to confine our
thinking to mere thinking, but we must also
have the courage to make that thinking come
true in reality.

#2

Acharya Chanakya said that -

" Destiny says that if you want to get more,
It will take a lot of risk to get more !
Some people do not take risks.
As life goes on, they just go on living.
But those who want to progress,

2

Those Who Want to rise above
What they have, they are
Not afraid to stake it,
Chances are that they will lose,
They will not be able to do anything,
But this attempt to do whatever it takes
to fulfil their dreams ,
This is what makes them
different from others !
And Even if they lose.
No one can snatch this satisfaction from them
That they have at least tried to do something
good. "

Meaning -

To get more, more from what we have now,
to achieve everything that we want, we will have
to work hard, and should be ready to face risks.
It is not necessary that we will always have to walk
on such a path which is safe, We will have to go
through such paths in life which are very risky and
difficult too.
" Because such paths are like the {Johri} jewellers
who carves the diamond. " By following such
paths, the person goes on embellishment.
Just like a clay pot has to be repeatedly hit with a
hand to give it the right shape, The pot is corrected
by hitting it in the right places where the correction
is needed. In exactly the same way, the difficult
path, which we are going to choose, that path will
definitely teach us a lot, About our mistakes, and
those mistakes will explain to us, and tell us how

3

much more hard work we need to do on ourselves. One such path will show us the right direction. Because a victory that has been achieved by walking on the path of struggles, the journey of which has been extremely difficult, such a victory is not only called a victory but that victory is always recalled as an historic victory. Which is always remembered even in the pages of history. And the succeeding generations also honour such a victory.

That is why it is very important that you should remember not to panic at all by walking on new paths. You should not be afraid to experience new things. Rather, we should welcome as many new experiences as we can and we should Accept them. And in this way, one should keep on composing the story of their own victory !

#3

Acharya Chanakya said that -

" Emperors are not born as emperors,
they have to be made into an emperor !
To create a united India, one has to dream first. "

Meaning -
No one is born as a king ! There is no person who knows all the art forms from his birth or he is skilled in everything from his birth !

To master any skill
Every human has to work very hard to achieve that art that he / she wants to master !
And it is also very important that the person gives time to that art properly and only then will he be able to master that art, that knowledge !
Because without effort,
Without practice,
No one can master anything !
And at the same time, Acharya Chanakya also told us that to create a united India, it is necessary to dream first of all, that is in order to master any art in the same manner, we should firstly have the knowledge related to that art.
And it is very important to know about that art even before gaining knowledge or mastering that art because
if you don't even know where to go ?,
In which direction to go ?
You will not be able to move !
Because a directionless person will just keep on wandering !
That's why A direction !
A Way !
Is a must !
Now the question arises that how will we know Which direction is meant for us ?
Which is our true path to success ?
Answer is simple - In order to find our true path, our true direction which is meant for us, we must always will have to be ready to listen to others as much as possible ! Our aim should be to gain

knowledge from other people's experiences, so that we don't repeat those mistakes that they did ! We will always have to be ready to acquire knowledge ! To learn whatever we can from whoever we can so that our knowledge increases to such an extant that we will eventually be able to take the right decisions !

Everything, every event that happens around us has to be taken care of in a way that has never been done before and to do that one will have to learn to be open to experiences , we will have to think about all the things like -

Is there such a thing or is there any such art, Whose practice can benefit me ?

What kind of learning can I benefit from ?

Is there anything in this text which can help me in a way that I will be able to grow and expand my knowledge ?

And it's not necessary that we must have all the answers prefeeded in our mind. We may have to find the answers to these questions. Maybe we can find these answers in someone's speech or in a text, or in a book.

But what is important is that we should not stop trying !

Only then will we be able to find our right path, And Will be able to move towards that direction, towards that path,

Which will lead us to our success.

#4

Acharya Chanakya said that -

" There are two paths for achieving the goals we
want to achieve in life .
A Simple and a difficult Way !
Simple route always attracts,
But it distracts us before reaching the goal.
But the difficult path, it can be long,
But it will surely lead us to our goal. "

(Many times it happens that over time the
meaning of said things starts changing.
That is why I have made some changes in the
meaning down below in translating the above said
lines by Acharya Chanakya and
I hope you too will agree with these changes. }

Meaning -

We have to make choices to achieve the goal,
Between the paths we feel are right for us.
Often the simplest route we think is right,
But it is not necessary that by going through a
simple/fixed route,
Only then can we get to our destination.
But it is also not necessary that we will definitely
reach our destination by going through the difficult
path. Or we can say that more than paths,
What is more important is to think about which
path will lead us to our destination, whether it is a
simple route or a difficult one.

It is more important to choose such a path
Which leads us to our goal. Whether it is a short
way or a long way. It is often the case that the
simple path that a person chooses to reach his/her
goal does not gives him/her the confidence that he/
she will be able to reach their desired goal.
But still people choose the same simple path and
are afraid to go on the difficult route !
Because they feel that walking on difficult path
will be a waste of their time. That Their hard work
will go in vain, but it is not so.
Because
" time and hard work are the two things in which if
we will invest they won't betray us ! "
And they will definitely lead us to our success !
It is necessary that we should know more than
what we already do to expand our knowledge !
And we should focus on the fact that how we will
be able achieve our goals ?
Rather than focusing on the difficulties that we are
possibly going to face by taking the difficult path !
Do you want to achieve a big goal in your life ?
And if that goal is so big then how can the path be
so simple ?
The bigger the goal, the harder the path.
Everyone likes to walk on easy roads, but can a
really easy road ever lead a person to a big life
changing point ?
No ! Right ?
It is clear from this very simple maths. That it is
not necessary that only a simple passage can lead
us to our destination. But just like two sides of a

coin, It's not necessary that the difficult path will definitely lead us to our destination !
But it is clear that whatever the route may be ,
In this game of paths,
Only The One will win who will be able to achieve his goal by facing all the difficulties and problems,
Because in the end, the route will not matter,
How many difficulties or troubles he/she has faced will not matter instead.....
In the end, all that will matter is whether the person is able to win or not, that whether he earns the victory he desires or not.

#5

Acharya Chanakya said that -

" The ideal student is one who under any circumstances,
Will Always be ready to learn,
Learn from small kids,
From elderly,
From anyone and everyone
His only goal is knowledge !
Whether he gets knowledge,
From strangers,
From friends,
Or from enemies.
His goal is simply learning at all costs !
Even if he gets respect or is insulted !
Learn whatever the teacher teaches

Do what your teacher says
You don't have to be behind anyone in learning. "

Meaning -

A student who is very serious about his work, his studies, his dreams, his goal, Such a student will never wastes his time.

He is always ready to learn under any circumstances.

Whether he gets education, from elder, from small kids, from friends or from his enemies,

Knowledge is paramount for such a student.

And Nothing else ! His goal is to learn only.

Whether he gets the honour or not.

Guru's order is everything for such a student.

Guru's command is a ladder for him that will help him reach his goals. His goal is not only to win but also to maintain the victory that he is going to achieve. Because many times people win, But after victory, they are unable to sustain that victory. And so they will ultimately have to face defeat.

Therefore, it is not only necessary to win, but to maintain that victory, you should be ready to learn in every situation ! Acknowledge your mistakes and never repeat them. And you should not let yourself be left behind in learning from anyone.

A person who is ready to learn in every situation, who is ready to accept his mistakes and is ready to improve, Only Such a person will be able to maintain his victory.

That is why this statement of Acharya Chanakya is very reasonable in every sense that anyone who

wants to achieve success, who has to win and
retain his victory,
He should never lag behind in learning from
anyone else. He should always be ready to learn to
accept knowledge from anyone and everyone !
Because his purpose is to use that knowledge for
good reasons and that is why his aim should only
be education at all cost !

#6

Acharya Chanakya said that -

" What is leadership ?
To fight the Enemy or the adversity ?
A good king
not only knows
How to attack
But he also knows
How to run when needed !
It also gives time to get organised.
There is No shame in running / leaving ! "

Meaning -

Acharya Chanakya here, were explaining to us the
meaning of leadership, that we should respect the
adverse circumstances. That is, a good king is not
the one who knows how to attack but he is the one
who knows how to retreat at the right time.
When you feel and when you are getting the hints
that you are going to lose, Then it is very

important to rectify your mistake and time is needed to rectify that mistake, we need to think about our shortcomings to build our strength. That time can only be found only then, When we retreat.

When in the battlefield do not get into a frenzy of anger but land there with complete preparation. Only then will you be able to achieve the victory that you desire for.

And even if you accidentally went to the battlefield without any preparation, it is better leave, to take time and to prepare and then when you get ready then you should go back to the battlefield.

There is nothing wrong in leaving the battle !
There is no harm in retreating !

With the retreat we will be able to get ready to attack again with a renewed vigour, with increased courage and good preparation. There should be no shame in retreat. It makes sense to retreat. When it is known that one will get defeated then retreating is the only solution !

If you heart still do not agree, remind him that we are not giving up ! We are just taking time. To make good preparations again !

For example, let's think that if a student has to take a test for an entrance and he has only one chance to attempt, only one attempt. And he knows that his preparations are not yet complete. And only a few days are left for that student's entrance exam, and even if that student goes to appear for the entrance exam, knowing that he has not done his preparation well then it is more likely that he will lose.

Because he did not prepare properly and at the same time this is his last chance. (Last Attempt !) Better than this, that student should study for a year with hard work and with a better strategy and then should give his last prompt to give that exam. Which will also increase the chances of him clearing that entrance exam.

Waiting for a year, studying, that student is not giving up, but he is accepting his mistakes that 'yes' he has not yet studied properly but now he is ready to rectify his mistake. By doing this, the student will also get time to prepare and also a better chance to win.

That is why it is very important to understand that there is no harm in retreat. Any shame Should not come. If we get this time by retreating to correct our mistake, to work on ourselves, to improve ourselves, then we should take that time. Such an opportunity should not be lost !

#7

Acharya Chanakya said that -

" Problem is not diagnosed in anger mania,
But with a quiet mind
Everyone can find a solution to the problem.
Always remember one thing,
Any destined problem is
not greater than Human capabilities.

The only problem is that most people don't face
their difficulties they run away from them.
But some people In the midst of difficulties,
Have the ability to achieve their goals.
Only his name is written in history.
One Who keep his goals in view
even in the most adverse circumstances,
who face their
Difficulties in the path of goal attainment without
getting entangled in their daily problems,
History is the witness, He has become great.
One who has made his difficulties
an opportunity to move forward.
Who's shortcomings have taught him how to use
them in his benefit,
He has always won the game "

Meaning -

Anger will never let you solve your problems. But
a calm mind can find a solution to every problem.
Because with a quiet mind we will be able to see
our problems clearly. Because there is no problem
that cannot be solved.

The only problem is that people give up before
solving the problem.

But some people consider it more appropriate to
try continuously instead of giving up.

Only a few people get success because they don't
stop their constant efforts.

While fighting with your inner dilemmas going on
in your inner self, Having Full faith in yourself,

You should keep trying and you will see how success comes to you !

Because even the burden of hardships will not be able to break those people who are willing not to give up under any circumstances.

The attention of such people is only focused towards their goal.

That is why Acharya Chanakya also advises that His difficulties should not be his weakness, but they should become his opportunities to move forward,

Your shortcomings should become your strength.

But how is this possible ?

How can anyone convert his shortcomings into his power ?

This can be done !

But how ?

I will explain it to you now.

We must first accept our shortcomings. Because if we do not accept our shortcomings then we will never be able to make them our strengths.

After accepting. We will have to work on those shortcomings. Either we can improve them by working on those deficiencies or we can build our strength.

Like if we are not very good in any one art, then by practicing that art, we can prepare ourselves in such a way, that we become proficient in that art.

That is, through continuous effort, we can master that art. You can make yourself capable by working hard on yourself.

This is the first way !

Another example can be that if a teacher wants to teach children but that teacher feels that he is not good at speaking, which is a very important requirement to become a teacher. So that teacher can educate children/students in writing. If that teacher is not good verbally he/she can teach students in textual written form.
Like writing books and writing his knowledge.
That is if you are not good at something then one can find other things in which they are good at and then make them his/her strength,
The point here is that one should focus on what they have and what they can work with !

#8

Acharya Chanakya said that -

" A true warrior is neither made up of physical
force, Nor from the knowledge of weapons,
You will Becomes a true warrior
Just by your intelligence !
The challenges will change in front of you.
You just need to focus on your goal !
So every challenge, every test
will definitely teach you something.
Acharya Chanakya had said that a true warrior
becomes one with his intellect. "

Meaning -
If we apply these lines in the student's lives,

It can be a very good example,
in the sense that if you try to implement it
That even if a student has physical force that is
The student may be healthy He may also have
knowledge of weapons, We can compare the
knowledge of Astra Shastra with bookish
knowledge, It may be that the student may has all
kinds of books needed to be proficient in the art or
subject or to master the art he wants to master,
but the most important thing What that student
should have is his intelligence.
That is even if you have everything what is needed
to be successful one will still have to apply those
things in his/her life or use those things according
to his/her needs intelligently !
We can also take another example-
That Even if a student does not have all the wealth
of the world, or the books which are needed for
him to be successful, he/she can still use his brain
and find a way by which he/she can arrange these
books or whatever is needed for him to achieve his
success,
Similar if we see the previous situation in that case
also even after having all the supplies or
ingredients needed for success one will have to put
them in order, to use them in an appropriate way so
that he will be able to achieve what he desires, in
this case even if a person has all the books he will
still have to read them himself.
He will have to use his intelligence on his own.
In spite of having the best books, if that student
does not study by himself.

That is, if he does not use his intelligence/mind, So it will be nothing but useless to have all those books he already has.

Because if a student will not work hard on his own, on himself, that is,

if he will not try to study himself, despite the conditions being in his favour, such a student will never be able to climb the ladder of success.

Acharya had also said that challenges will come one after another, changing their clothes/in different forms,

But our focus should not deter and should always be on our target.

Because if this happens, those challenges will definitely teach us something !

There may be some students who do not have all the facilities needed, Those who do not have money Or other things needed for their success But this is their confidence and their will power Which will help them to focus on their goal.

The needs of that student will motivate him to work hard, to prove and to show his best version to the world,

Not for anyone else but for himself.

So that when he stands in front of the mirror,

He will be proud of the hard work,

he will be proud of himself that wherever

he is today, he is due to his reason, due to his hard work, dedication and true desire to achieve his knowledge !

#9

Acharya Chanakya said that -

" What is the identity of a great warrior ?
When they won the war
Instead of wasting their time in
{Vijay Utsav} celebrations they start making plans
to achieve their next goal. "

Meaning -

After getting victory in the war, instead of getting
intoxicated in celebrations of that victory. It is
better to start working towards your next objective.
Because your real purpose, your real success will
not depend on one victory,
But to be truly successful, you will have to keep
trying continuously,
" You will have to win again and again. "
And every time you will have to prove your worth
by winning through new challenges. That you are
worthy of this success. Otherwise, history is the
witness that most of the deceit happens to the
people who lost their time in celebrations of their
victory.
If you too are going to be lost in your celebrations
you will find the real purpose of your life different
from yourself, thus it is very important for you to
keep track of your time in order to sustain your
victory, your success, one must always be
focused !

Because if you will keep wandering and celebrating then you will reach nowhere, and you will surely have to see the face of defeat.

#10

Acharya Chanakya said that -

" As long as the smouldering fire
is under our control,
Till then we can use it.
But if the fire breaks out of our control,
It will destroys everything and
causes the apocalypse.
That's why, be patient. "

Meaning -
Acharya Chanakya meant that
anger is just like the burning fire. If we give
direction to our anger, to our burning fire and if we
divert that anger to our efforts, to our own benefits,
divert it towards our goals, then even that anger
can be useful for us, it can be used to motivate us,
to fuel us in the direction of our dreams !
But if the same anger, is not used wisely and it gets
out of control, That is if we could not handle that
anger, that fire within us, beneath us then it can be
the cause of our own destruction !

That is if we do not control that anger, but if that anger controls us, then such an anger, Will prove to be more harmful to us than anyone else.

The fire of such an anger can only invite an apocalypse, An apocalypse of our own world !

That is why it is very important that we understand, that no matter how angry we are, we can use that anger in the right direction. for example - If there is a student whose teachers scold him a lot, And say to him - that you will never be able to do anything in your life !

Anger is inevitable when such a student is not encouraged to work hard on himself/herself and he/she only gets the angry from his/her teachers.

Then In such a situation that student will have two options. One is that either that student can become angry and quit his/her studies,

Or the second and the most wise choice is to use his anger as his fuel which will give him the courage to be bold and face all the difficult situations in his life as well as it will give him the courage to face the reality and the world by working on himself, in order to become the better version of himself, that he wants to be !

And in order to do so, One must use his anger in a controlled and focused way, he must divert this energy that he is going to gain from his anger into something useful and productive !

And should keep this in his mind that he's not doing these things to impress anyone but he's doing this so that he can use his abilities to his full potential ! So that he will also be able to show his teachers that He is not one of those who succumb to the circumstances, but he is one of those who have the ability to win by facing the circumstances.

#11

Acharya Chanakya said that -

" Whenever people change their
behaviour towards you,
be very careful with them.
People who praise without reason
are like poison covered with milk.
You need to be aware of them. "

Meaning -
Many times we too would have expected some kind of behaviour from people at some point in our life, but their behaviour changes towards us suddenly which makes us wonder, We think those people have changed.
Maybe They want good for us but it's not what it looks like !
No one can change without any reason or purpose. In fact " change in itself means converting from one form to another, to become a different version of you by not being the same version of you which you were before but by still being you ! "
In very rare circumstances it happens that someone's behaviour is true to us when it has changed suddenly. Like after a close friendship.

But it is most likely that human behaviour changes with reasons, it changes for its own sake. That is why it is very important to distinguish who is your own real friend and who is acting like one !

#12

Acharya Chanakya said that -

" When a person forgets to
distinguish between friend and foe,
understand that he has taken
his first step towards his downfall. "

Meaning -
Who is our friend ?
And who is our enemy ?
How will the difference between it will be understood ?
To understand these differences, people often look at the behaviour of the people around them, but the behaviour can be changed.
It can be changed in such a way that we will only be able to see what that person wants to show us, so it is not necessary that someone's behaviour will clearly show that he is our friend or an enemy.
Now the question arises how to find out who is our friend and who is our enemy ?
There is only one way to find this out and that is,
" If one stop seeing the mirror
but instead look for the reflection,

then one may find the true appearance ! "
That is if we stop predicting someone's attitude
towards us with respect to the mirror shown to us
or their behaviour, then and then only we will be
able to see their true self through their reflection or
the reason/belief/purpose behind their behaviour !
If we stop accepting what is shown to us, instead
start finding and asking questions about what could
be the reason/purpose behind this person's
behaviour towards us, then we will be able to find
the answers we are looking for.

#13

Acharya Chanakya said that -

" There is no challenge to walk with those
who have already accepted you as their leader !
The challenge is to carry them along,
Who doesn't consider you their leader ! "

Meaning -
Those who are your friends, they will always
support you, it is not difficult to get the support of
your friends. But you should get support from
those who oppose you.
Because if the opposing party joins you, your
victory will be guaranteed !
Now the usual question arrives will it not be a risk
to keep a enemy so close ?
No !

There is a very common saying.
" Keep your friends close and your enemies even closer. "
When those enemies stay with you. And when they will see how good your behaviour is towards them. What good things you do and what a good person you are. In real life instead of the people with whom they have lived before.
So they too will understand this, acknowledged this that their support should go to the right person.

#14

Acharya Chanakya said that -

" Listen to everyone,
But do what you feel like !
and one more thing
A friend or an enemy,
All can be won with love. "

Meaning -

All can be won by love, It is also possible that we may start getting support from our enemies.
Seeing our good behaviour, our generosity and truth they may realise that they are on the wrong side.
Love can heal, it can mend it has the truth and a true and a real power which can even rebound a broken heart.

Acharya also said that one should listen to everyone whether a suggestion is given by his friend or by an enemy, because then one can notice whether other people are trying to implant planned thoughts in his mind or are they really trying to help, one may also notice the fact that who's on his side and who's not ! But one will always have to take his own decisions !

That is, in any situation, no matter what the problem is, the decision should be taken by one's own thinking and not by someone else's.

It is not necessary that the one who is your friend today, will still be your friend tomorrow. Also He may be an enemy in disguise wearing costume of a friend and it is also not necessary that who we consider our enemy would actually be our enemy. It is very difficult to distinguish between an enemy and a friend.

" What we can see is for sure is happening, but what we cannot is also happening ! "

Evidence of one's truth, good or evil,

In this Kali-yuga, (modern world)

No one can see or tell by listening to his words/or by what the other person has to say.

That is why it is necessary that whatever decision we take, it should be a product of our own thinking and not by being influenced by someone else's thoughts, in order to prevent this one must be aware of every thought, of your friends and of your enemies too.

#15

Acharya Chanakya said that -

" There is a difference between
good and bad people.
What happens is that sometimes
good people teach a lesson to the bad people they
Forget the basic goodness of their soul.
They become just like those bad people.
Therefore One Must Always remember
this fine difference.
Because this difference
also saves humans from being an animals.
'Yes', You should teach the bad people,
the lesson they deserve,
but don't become an animal while doing so. "

Meaning -

Many times we get cheated on friendship too.
And then the mind becomes rage to avenge this
deception.
But is revenge everything ?
Can't that person be forgiven ?
Is it fair to waste your time on the person who
cheated on you ? Is that person, that fraudulent
person is so important to you that you will allow
that person to eat more of your time and your life ?
Also It is not necessary to take revenge in every
situation !

Many times it happens that a person perceives cheating and an inappropriate behaviour as equal. Both are quite the opposite actually !

Cheating means betrayal, you can think about it whether there is a need to take action against it or not, according to situations and the circumstances one can decide.

But an Inappropriate behaviour can not be tolerated, ie, if a teacher slaps a student, So that is an inappropriate behaviour. One should raise voice against such behaviour. Such a behaviour cannot be tolerated. Against them, complaint should also be made to the school principal/ higher authorities, also involving parents in such a situation is a must !

Most of the times in life, It is a fact that our loved ones are the ones who would have done wrong with us. That is the time when our patience and honesty gets tested, we will have to prove that we are right to stand for what is right,

When we will have to raise our voice, we will have to speak against the wrong and dare.

So that that wrong cannot be repeated again with anyone.

And if you Don't want to see yourself in the mirror like a loser, But like a courageous person then you will have to stand up and fight against all the odds !

And learn to raise your voice against injustice !

Learn to face the wrong. But not by taking law and justice in our own hands, but by staying within our limits and by doing the right thing.

#16

Acharya Chanakya said that -

" The leader is the one
who carries every member of the party along.
Take proper use of their abilities.
And achieve the desired goals
while facing every situation ! "

Meaning -

Every member of the team should be taken along.
Like if a student has been given some group work,
and if he is the leader of that team/of his group.
So that student according to the abilities of all the
students of his group should distribute work
amongst them according to their capabilities !
The incharge of that group should distribute the
work in the group according to their specialities so
that their group/team can pass in the given work.
That is students should have an understanding of
what work to give to whom. According to the
abilities of the people. That is work should be
discussed and then distributed considering the fact
that what exactly are the things in which they are
good at, one should not do partiality, by choosing
friendship over the right decision which they know
they should take, because such an action may
increase their chances of failure !
Because if you really want to achieve your goal,
suppose in this case, one may want to excel,

In his class with good numbers, good scores and If you want to come first and get full marks in your group work, then everyone has to work together and should work according to their specialities ! Because these specialists and these characteristics are the ones that makes us all different from each other, and with the help these different characteristics one can become successful in any task.

#17

Acharya Chanakya said that -

" Friends are not made. They are earned ! "

Meaning -

Our real friends are made, when we have seen or experienced their circumstances very closely ourselves.

In such a way that we can see them going through the same path as we did before, only then one can feel and relate to the problems of another.

Because then your friend becomes your guide, as they both knows what it feels like while being in a certain situation, When one experiences another, only then they can have the title of a true friendship.

Just like when sun shines and shows everyone the right way, the right path, similarly such a friendship will lead them to the path of their success.

Respecting the circumstances of any friend, preventing them from wandering the wrong path, showing them the right direction, no matter what, When such a brotherly love is between two friends. So that will be a real friendship !
Which is not impossible in this Kali-yuga, (modern world) But it is rarely seen and is much more valuable than anything.

Such a true friendship, gives courage to a person, will encourage him to do good work.

And will motivate him to not to go on the wrong path, because when One person builds trust in another person, Then not only one but two brains starts working together. They start working in the same direction with different opinions and tactics, and then the direction which is found, it cannot be wrong, it will be the ultimate path.

Because every person has different thoughts, different ways of thinking, handling and coping up even with the same situation, so these different thoughts and different perspectives will definitely help you to find the right path which is meant for you !

So real friends are not made, they are earned by helping them, when in need, by understanding their circumstances, by thinking with the right ideology. And showing each other the right path with truth and goodness.

#18

Acharya Chanakya said that -

" There is no greater joy than enlightenment.
There is no disease greater than sexuality.
and No enemy greater than physical attraction "

Meaning -

Knowledge of the soul is paramount. To know that
we are born for a purpose.

We were born to fulfil any one objective in our
lives, which will result in good not only for
ourselves but also for the whole world, for the
whole humanity,

So such an enlightenment will keep us from the
mark of ignorance,

Will give us the power to move forward to reach
our goals and will also motivation us from within.

Regarding sexuality and physical attraction,
Acharya has said that sexuality is the
greatest enemy of the human being because it only
distracts us from the right path,

The first goal in a student's life should be that they
should firstly get education by reading and writing.

They should do something for the whole human
race.

This target/aim may sound very big but we will
have to think big, in order to really achieve
something big.

Because if we don't think then we will never be
able to do it. And the bigger the goal, the harder

the path and you will have to work as hard as possible to achieve the goal that you are dreaming of today.

" Therefore, before the external enemy, you must fight and defeat the internal enemies. "

i.e Attraction and sexuality, which is just a product of our own mind if we stop getting dissolved in these temptations from our mind then nothing will be able to deter us !

Because if we won't fight these temptations then they will surely try to trap us.

But we do not have to get carried away by those thoughts.

Your focus should always be on your target, just like Arjun, that when his guru asked him,

What do you see ?

So the answer should always be that I only see my goal and nothing else.

Only the eye of the fish and nothing else.

And your determination towards your goal should be so strong that even your own thoughts won't be able to distract you and your mind should be so focused towards your goal that even if someone tries to fill you with unnecessary, unproductive rubbish even then those thoughts won't break you,

" when your heart stops dominating your mind only then you will get this incredible sense of focus towards your goal "

because when this happens only then you will be able to achieve your desired goal.

#19

Acharya Chanakya said that -

" No person is exceptionally intelligent !
A person is either intelligent or foolish.
What is extraordinary in this ?
We are all normal human beings.
They are just like us ! "

Meaning -
When Acharya Chanakya's disciple praised his
enemy, he told acharya that their enemy was
extraordinary. And he has always been winning.
So Acharya explained to his disciple that no person
is extraordinary. He is either intelligent or stupid.
Who knows how to get his work done, who knows
how to climb the ladder of success, Often people
do not get tired of praising such a person.
And these mere talks grow so much that,
that person starts getting looked up upon as an
extraordinary person. But he is not extraordinary.
He only knows the right path to reach his victory.
He knows about the right direction, He knows how
he has to adapt to the circumstances and how to
win.
A person who loses, even if he has some ability, no
one will praise him because nobody praises a loser.
What does it means, it means to make yourself so
capable, to mold yourself in such a way that no
matter how many people have the guide, the key to
success, to secret,

But success should always be yours to keep,
But how is that possible ?
That is for sure is possible, only if you don't run
from your problems, you face them with courage
and win over them with confidence !
Because only you can determine your own path of
victory and no one else can !
Because efforts made with determination will
never let you fail !
Whether you get success or not, But there will be
always a lot to learn, Which will prevents us from
repeating those mistakes and will provide us the
ability to see our situations in a new way, with a
new thinking.
Therefore, One should always strive for success.
And at the same time one should not believe in
imaginary things such as someone being
extraordinary.

#20

Acharya Chanakya said that -

" If you know your words,
you know yourself and your enemy,
So you will not get afraid
from the result of <u>100</u> wars;
If you know yourself
but you don't know your enemy,
So you should always be ready for
defeat with victory.

But if you do not know your enemy and
neither do you know yourself,
So you will always have to be ready
to see your defeat. "

Meaning -

To win you will not only need to know yourself
but you should also be aware of the moves which
are taken by your enemy. That is, you must know
your shortcomings as well as the strengths of
others. So that measures can be taken to deal with
their strengths and also one should work on their
own weaknesses.

About these policies, regarding how to get victory
over your enemies, how to face their rage and
moves we will talk in detail in Chanakya Neeti
Part 2, but for now from a student's perspective,
A student should know this that along with his
shortcomings, that what other things are the other
students of his class are doing ?

Are they getting more marks than you or are they
scoring less than you ? You need to know about
both the sides of a coin for example if their marks
are less than your marks then you should learn
from their mistakes and should not repeat their
mistakes, like if some one is getting less marks due
to not studying properly, one can learn from such a
student to learn and give time to his studies
properly, one should not make those mistakes
which other students are doing which are costing
them their marks, in order to maintain your success

one must know everything not just only about
winning but about loosing too.

or if others are scoring more than what you are
scoring then you should learn from those students,
you should notice and ask them what is it that they
are doing differently, what is it that is making them
score more marks ?

Whether it is because they are reading more books,
or because they are attending tuition. Or because
of the fact that they are studying for more than two
hours daily, you should find these answers and you
should also adopt the same policies in order to
excel !

So Along with being aware of yourself, it is also
very important to have all the information about
the enemy side as well. Then whether they are
losing or winning. Because this information is
more valuable than winning or loosing, as this
information can teach you those lessons which will
help you in your entire life.

" Because knowledge will always be the real
wealth in any era ! "

#21

Acharya Chanakya said that -

" The appropriate choice must be made
at the appropriate time.
Only He will survive in a crisis
who has adapted himself to the circumstances. "

Meaning -

This means that your choices, will determine what your results will be, Will your objective be successful or not ? Even at the time of crisis, when the destiny will be taking your test, your decisions at that moment will show that, how well you are able to handle the pressure and how well will you be able to cope up with the situation, your way of dealing with your situations will determine your path to success.

If you really want to win, then you will have to understand that victory is meant only for those people who are ready to adapt to the circumstances, to the situations,

One who accepts his mistakes and does not repeat those mistakes again, Who confesses that 'yes', he has made mistakes so far but now he is ready to work on himself, only such a person will face success.

If we understand this sentence in more detail, adapted to the circumstances, then it will also makes us understand that no matter what the problem is, the solution to solve that problem is always going to be in that problem, no matter how hard or difficult the problem may look like but the solution is always there, we just need to focus and then we will be able to find it !

Everyone must have heard that

" Where straightforwardness has never a chance of working, crookedness flourishes. "

that is, exactly in the same way if we are unable to solve any problem then we should look at the problem with other people's perspective or with their point of view, think of the problem as if suppose this or that person would have faced this problem, what would they have done to come out of it ? What would have been their move if they were in this problem ? How would they have solved this problem ?

" One will have to change their own perspectives, in order to find different solutions for the same problem ! "

#22

" Once, while walking in the path, Acharya Chanakya's leg got pierced by a thorn from a spongy bush. So he said that - The trouble I suffered, That should not happen to others, so It is necessary to destroy the cause of this suffering. So the disciple of Acharya Chanakya asked, how will this suffering be destroyed by putting buttermilk in this bush ? Acharya replied - Buttermilk in this bush is an open invitation to those ants who will now come and eradicate the bush from it's roots. After that, this path will be cleared for everyone. It is not necessary to avoid the problem. The sensible is the one who runs into the problem and then eradicates it. "

Meaning -

Running away from your problems is not the way to win over any problem. If we want to win over the problem, to end that problem forever, then it is necessary that we face that problem.

The problem will have to be faced with such a courage, in such a way that the problem does not arise ever again and never again we get lost from our right path.

Acharya did not only helped himself by putting buttermilk in that bush, but he made that path clear and free of thorns for everyone.

He not only thought for himself but for everyone and that is what makes Acharya so special.

If he would have left from there by just thinking about himself, then he could have easily avoided that problem but he remained there, thought a solution to remove that problem forever so that it won't harm anyone else.

That is, The rest of the people who would have walked on the same path would also have to go through the same pain.

That is why, after thinking about them,
he poured buttermilk in that bush, In exactly the same way, we too should not think only about ourselves,

But we should think about everyone. Because the one who does good to everyone, destiny also rewards him with good fruits.

#23

Acharya Chanakya said that -

" Whenever you make a plan,
And if it succeeds.
So how do you get out of it ?
Always remember this side. "

Meaning -

It is very important to think not only about the
success of any task, but also about our first step
after that success. Because only the first step after
that success will show whether we will be able to
maintain that success or not.

And towards this step, the first step to be taken
after success is also the recognition that if those
steps are taken in the right direction then the
success will remain. At the same time, we will be
able to move faster towards our set target, but if
those steps go towards wrong paths, we might not.
be able to maintain our success, the dangers of
getting lost and distracted from our right path will
continue to hover.

For example, if a student has successfully given
his school exams, then after his exams,
he should think about his next step in advance, i.e
without wasting his time he should focus on his
next task. He should start studying for his next
purpose, he should start his preparations for
achieving his next goal.

Another example of this can also be, suppose if a student has successfully finished his 12th class with a good rank, but he got so dissolved in his success that he completely forgot to apply for entrance exam and now he does not know in which direction he has to go, after achieving his success, That is, after attaining the desired result, it is also very important to think in which direction one should go next and which step one will take ? Because if we don't think about these things in advance and when time will demand our attention, so we will be so entangled in our own dilemmas and maybe due to this we would take the wrong decision. As in this example. Already, that student, due to not being aware of the entrance exam or for the reason that he forgot, he made a mistake, by not taking the right decision at the right time, which costed him his academic year.

For example if someone wants to become an engineer, then he/she will have to give the JEE exam. Similarly for every goal a path is already fixed, no one knows the exact way to achieve his/her goal in the exact way, but references will always be there which will help us in showing the right path.

That is before going through any challenge, you should known exactly what will you do after winning, after achieving the desired results, what is your next move going to be ? Which path will you move on and in which direction ?

#24

Acharya Chanakya said that -

" We should not unnecessarily shrink
with our past.
Nor should we be unduly anxious
about our future.
The present is true.
There should be complete focus on the same.
But how ?
Gain strength from the past
and build your present
by being in the present moment.
The future will be set automatically. "

Meaning -

Forget what happened, leave worrying about what
is going to happen.
Focus only on the present !
Because we cannot change the past.
Even if a student has made a mistake, he will
eventually emerge from that mistake.
But now it is not the time to regret it.
This is the time of repentance, to correct our
mistakes, not to cover up what we have done, but
to accept it.
To move forward. And that can happen only and
only when we live in the present.
Do not think about your mistakes again and again
Let the past be in the past. And today, start a new
with new pages.

Forgetting the past, Put in more thinking today. And at the same time, we should not be too anxious about the future. Because we do not know what could happen in the future.

What we thought if that didn't happen, then our dreams will be shattered and when this happens, with those shattered dreams what breaks along is the confidence of that human.

Our own self-confidence should not be broken, so that we can be ready for any situation.

Be prepared to face all things, whether good or bad. So whatever you think or dream of, make sure that you work towards that goal or those dreams of yours might always stay away from your reality, And that future that you are worried about, it should be created by you now, by living in the now.

But how will you create your future ?

It is very important to evaluate the present situation in order for one to be read for the future. One should learn from his past, live in the present and act accordingly.

Further to evaluate the situation where one is now, one should be prepared to face even the crises which may arise or one should be prepared for the possible problems he/she is about to encounter, because if one will be prepared to face all the obstacles in advance then he/she will be able to reach his/her desired goal without being lost in the way with much more focus.

#25

Acharya Chanakya said that -

" Time is priceless. Don't waste it like this. "

Meaning -

Time is often understood only by the people who have lost their time. Time is very precious. What is the importance of time in a student's life ?

Only one such student can explain this to another student who had wasted his time and maybe because of wasting his time he would have scored less marks.

Because remorse is the only thing that teaches us to appreciate what we had lost, what we don't have, i.e time. A person who has gone through that suffering who has faced that pain only that person can tell you what he has lost because he knows more than two moments of happiness, that is by wasting his time he knows what he has lost and how precious it was.

Only one such student can explain the pain of that suffering very easily. In words that no other person could understand, not even the person who has used his time perfectly.

That is why if you want to know the importance of time correctly, ask those people about their experiences who have actually experienced it. About their school time stories. And I know for sure that in more than one of their stories, you will definitely get to know the importance of time.

Today, we take time for granted, because we do not know about its pricelessness.

Being Priceless means you cannot evaluate it's value. Something which when gone it cannot be reproduced. The one who will not use his/her time appropriately will end up with nothing but with repentance and sadness.

So in a student's life, one should use his time properly. A student should be disciplined in such a way that there will be no need to remind him the importance of time again and again. And whenever he wastes his time, he should be determined enough that he can understand from himself that he is making a mistake. By doing such a mistake he will loose whatever he has earned till date and will be forced to accept his defeat.

#26

Acharya Chanakya said that -

" The key to success lies in focusing
on your stated goal.
Do Not get entangled in such things
which will lead you to problems. "

Meaning -

It is very important in the life of a student not to waste his time in such things about which he know that they will waste his time. After which he could not get anything other than repentance and torture in the end. Time is very valuable in the life of a student. It is the time when he has to learn.

If he is going to dedicate that time to his studies with all truth, loyalty and dedication, then he will definitely able to become someone, in his life.

He will be able to do anything that he wants to achieve, But if he gets entangled in useless things then he will never be able to do anything and will not be able to make anything useful out of his life.

For example -

What are the obstacles in a student's life that confuse him ?

There may be many such things, such as
those students who stop learning,
do that because

- Either they fall in love, or
- They start wasting their time in fights or
- The race to become teacher's spoon/ his/her favourite in the classroom.
- Or the rush to get a recognised as the class monitor !

In the minds of many students. Questions must be arising as to why becoming a class monitor is not right ? Just think what It means to become a class monitor. Spending the whole day's energy on other student's. To lose your energy by screaming.

At the end of the day, one will come home and will feel so tired, as if someone would have forced you to break bricks and stones.

Often to calm the students our teachers send us to the classes of young children to calm them down. They want pin drop silence in their class and we all know how much impossible it is to create silence

in the classroom which is full of primary class students.
Is very difficult. More than any entrance exam ! Their energy level is much more than an adult or teenage student. And even if some of them are not very naughty, it is not in their dictionary to listen and do what is said. And at the same time, we sometimes get such teachers those who stop us from taking their own class and will send the monitor to mind the class of primary children, as if that student is being paid to do so, as if he/she has enrolled in school just so that they can quite others and maintain silence,
You will not be able to read and learn and will eventually be forced to miss your classes because you will be put to work, teachers will force you to go for minding the students, " To pacify someone else which is not your job at all. "
And if those children do not calm down then you will be accused of what you were doing there ? Why couldn't you calm them down ? The point is that either you can take education in school or you can do this forced labour work of monitoring the children. Either time can be wasted by getting submerged into a title like the class monitor or you can study and learn and do the things for which you actually go to school for.
You have to make this decision on your own.
But from my point of view it is very useless to be a class monitor due to these few reasons. As well as fighting other pupils in a frenzy of rage which is another way to waste your time. And getting entangled in things like love can also create

obstacles in the path of achieving your dreams and your education.

Because these things in the end will affect a student's life very badly and will only prove to be the medium to distract the mind.

That's why one should focus and Get involved in making plans and working on them rather than getting into messy things.

And therefore your first goal should be that you should study with your whole heart and pay attention to the things which matter the most to you. Your eyes should only be on your goals and nowhere else !

#27

Acharya Chanakya said that -

" To do any big task.
Only proper planning is not necessary.
That plan also requires complete faith.
If plan is very good, So the decisions that will complete the campaign will also be good.
That's why old knowledgeable people had said, Good plans can also make impossible
-looking dreams come alive. "

Meaning -

If we make a plan for any major task today and we do not believe in that plan. So somewhere we will not be able to work on that plan with our full potential or with our full dedication in that plan, so it is very important that If you have a plan, then you must trust it too. And believe it enough to make it come true. Put all your strength to complete it. Put your whole life to it, because if you believe then only you will be able to achieve what you want to achieve.

Also your plans should be accurate and precise because good plans bring good results. So it is very important that whenever you make a plan, it should also be good.

But how will we know whether the plan that we have prepared is correct or not ?

We will have to inspect that plan ourselves, but if for some reason we do not understand and are having difficulty in understanding whether our plan is right or not, then do not be afraid to ask questions. One should not be afraid of what other people will think, about us.

You will have to be bold enough to take risks, to ask questions you want to know the answer of, maybe you will have to take the opinion of some of your elders or you will have to ask someone for their advice, but what is fixed is that you will have to try because that's the only way.

You will have to look at your plan from someone else's point of view, so that you can clearly see whether your plan will take you closer to your success, closer to your set goal or not.

So whenever you plan take opinions, ask questions and also you should try to look at that plan from a different perspective, from a different direction so that plan never fails.

#28

Acharya Chanakya said that -

" Whenever I make a plan,
doubts remain in my mind about its success.
I try to bring the vision of the plan to work with
my experiences and insight, keeping in mind the
potential crisis that could occur. But the success of
the work is decided by mixed efforts of plan,
fortune and conscience. All three have an equal
role in the success of the work. "

Meaning -

Acharya Chanakya also had doubts about the plan.
In order to clear the doubts, they used to think
about the scheme's vision, that is, the way in which
the plan will take shape into reality, the possible
crises which could occur and with the help of their
experience and insights, they made the plan so
efficient that the plan would for surely take them to
their intended goal.

But still the success of the work also depends on
how those plans are made. Whether the plan has
been made very well or not, as well as destiny and
conscience and thought potential also plays
important role, Considering every viewpoint that
what could happen ?

What are the possible obstacles ?

Who can cause these obstacles ?

The final stage of planning can be reached by
thinking about all these things.

By focusing on all these things, the final stage of planning can lead us to our desired end goal. Because the final stage of any plan is the main decision maker it decides the outcome of the set plan.

Therefore, the last step should be such that our victory is guaranteed.

For example - If a student creates a time table to study. The time limit for that student determines that at this time, that student will have to study a particular subject and then after that a different subject and so on, then what usually happens is that in the beginning, he does all the things.

That is, in the initial time, he reads all the subjects very well. But in the end, as his will power and his enthusiasm gets reduced, such thoughts start coming in his mind that he has a choice he can just read later, those ideas should not come, because such thoughts are the roots of distraction and so even at that time when we don't want to study and Considering other possible ways of spending our time, even at that time we will have to be strong about our plan, about our desired goals and our path, but that can only happen when the plans are so well designed that distraction won't even matter. Then they won't be able to misguide us even when we forget the main cause of why we are studying in the first place, those plans those strict timetables, those habits of being responsible won't let us go the wrong path and will always guide us. but when does our mind start playing with us exactly ? when does we start forgetting that what we have started was for a cause, our mind does that when we are tired, main reason being that we won't let ourselves rest, and so it is very important that after 1 to 2 hours of study, everyone should take a break for some time or stop studying .

It becomes necessary for our brain to process the information that is being feed-ed because the purpose of education should not be to mug up things but to understand them in such a way that those concepts, those topics stays with us forever.

now the question which is going to be raised is that what one should do in this break time exactly, one must utilise this time, one can spend that time in an activity/exercise so that his/her body also remains healthy and active, because as we know long hours of continuous studying will also make us lazy and will eventually give us a back pain for free, moreover

because of sports/activities one will be able to keep his mind in studies, these activities will work as refreshments for the brain, otherwise all day those thoughts which distract us from our right path when they will come to our mind we will be forced to quit, or we can diminish their existence by being highly motivated and relaxed while studying by giving time to extra curricular activities.

This is the main reason as to why we should distribute our time properly for every activity in a day so that we can focus all our attention on that one thing which matters the most to us and which will enable us to reach our desired goals.

That is why our time table should be practical.
It should be real, not fake,

because sometimes we know, we won't be able to complete certain tasks/the so called dream timetables we make but we still keep making those fake timetable which for the moment Will satisfy our ego that we have done something productive but in reality we would still have a lot to do, for example some children will make impossible and fake time tables that they will wake up at 6:00 am and study continuously till 12:00 pm, they would write all the impractical stuff in that time table which they actually know they won't be able to complete in reality and which is a blatant white lie.

Every student should stop studying after 1/or2 hours or according to their capabilities they should take break or some time interval for curricular activities between studies.

One should do this so that they do not get exhausted at all because of boredom with studies. That is why giving yourself enough breaks for your mind to breathe and relax to consume more knowledge along with making real time table is very important.

Or we can say that it is necessary to make real plans and not schemes that are impossible which cannot be fulfilled, Only then will we have full faith in that plan and only then will we dedicate our entire attention to that plan and will be able to give our 100%.

#29

Acharya Chanakya said that -

" Every great dream begins with the person who
dreams, But the dreamer must always remember
that to fulfil his dreams,
Willpower and persistence lies within him.
Which will reach the planets and constellations
and will lead his whole world to change.
One more thing,
Not all thoughts suddenly come to life.
Not all dreams suddenly take tangible form.
For this, the person should be
on a pedestal of patience.
One has to be patient !
Because when destiny breaks the pace of events.
So it should be understood that she is giving us the
signal to wait for the right opportunity.
So never leave patience. "

Meaning -
Everyone sees dreams,
but
how many people are there who will fulfil these
dreams ?
only a few, right ?
Why is it that only a few people can fulfil their
dreams while others won't ?
that's because Not everyone has the same
determination and will to achieve those dreams,

to fulfil their dreams one will require hard work, perseverance, will power and apart from that, trust and patience is also required. Therefore it is very important to maintain moderation and patience because when destiny breaks the pace of events. At that time she wants to indicate to us that we need to wait for the right time.

Because there are some decisions that we understand when we come to an age. In exactly the same way, how a student sees love the way it is understood by the student's the way he/she experience it, it's meaning will change a lot as that student grows older and become smarter, the meaning of love, that understanding will drastically change from what he/she already knew, because as we grow up, our intelligence also grows, our perceptions change, opinions enhances, and eventually everyone will notice that you will change and become completely different from what you used to be just with your experiences and with your age and then finally one day you will start to understand things differently.

#30

Acharya Chanakya said that -

" If you want fruit in a year, sow rice,
if your plan is for 10 years, then plant a tree,
but if you want a plan for lifetime,
then educate people. "

Meaning -

If fruit is needed in one year, grow rice crop. If there is a plan for 10 years, grow trees, but if the plan is to last a lifetime, then educate people because they will educate people further and this education will provide such knowledge to all, that any person will not be able to remain uneducated or deprived of education, but the glory of education will light this world and will remove darkness.

Because if people are not educated then they will listen or believe in any kind of things and sometimes some people misuse the faith and the facts that other people aren't aware of that is why it is very important for people to be educated and the entire human race should be made aware of the ocean of knowledge. They should be explained that education has real power.

Because education is the medium through which a person can understand the distinction between right and wrong. He understands that in which direction we have to move and why. Both the meaning and the purpose in life comes from education.

And thus education will create such ideas and thoughts which will be capable of bringing change in the society, the society will be able to know and understand and will be encouraged to stand up for the rights things which matters to them as these thoughts cannot be defeated by evil because these thoughts are immortal, these thoughts will be

educated enough to decide what's right and what's
wrong they will be able to distinguish the
distinguishable and then and only then people will
realise the power of truth and how important it is
to stand up for what is right.
Therefore a sensible man should understand that
while helping other humans with his knowledge,
they should also be made aware of this knowledge.
They should be taught to do things themselves,
so that knowledge can go forward and expand to
guide everyone in the future.

#31

Acharya Chanakya said that -

" If defeat happens, if a person is defeated,
he can try again for victory.
When he accepts defeat with the mind,
then only he is defeated.
Many times those who accept defeat by heart.
To those it is not known,
That when they gave up the courage.
How close were they to their victory then !
Every defeat which comes in the way of your
journey. It is just an experience.
Such an experience which will teach you a lesson,
Our shortcomings makes us better they teaches us
our mistakes, they takes us closer to our victory by
correcting us, by improving us day by day. "

Meaning -

Unless a person accepts his defeat with his mind, he cannot be defeated. He is not declared a loser until he gives up.

This is to say that one should keep striving continuously for victory. Because many times people who have accepted their defeat they don't know how close they were to their victory when they gave up,

And only one wrong decisions is all that takes which drove them away from victory forever, they themselves destroyed, their chances of winning.

By thinking that they have lost, assuming they have lost and deciding that they will no longer try, they made a huge mistake.

The mistake which they committed costed them their victory.

The number of times a person loses, The number of times one has to see the face of defeat, at that time, that person experiences something that he does not know about, he gets to know about new things. He realises his mistakes, he reconsiders everything and tries to improve himself by knowing and accepting his shortcomings and rectifying them, so that those mistakes won't hinder him again when he'll be set to conquer his victory.

If a person wants to try again, by daring to win again, he can dare to continue. But after losing something they had, they lose faith in themselves and they do not make any effort. And then finally give up, saying it wasn't in their luck, destiny, they make excuses to cover up for what they have lost, they try to satisfy their brain with what they have, but deep inside their heart they know what they have lost, they know that they have replenished their last chance by not letting themselves try, by forcing themselves to get confined in their own boundary.

But if the path of victory was so simple, then today everyone would have been successful. Yes, the path to success is not that simple, but is not impossible as well, to achieve victory, one has to make constant efforts, only then will he be able to reach his desired destination.

#32

Acharya Chanakya said that -

" What is an impossible-looking decision ?
One such difficult decision which can be taken.
So take the decision
no matter how impossible it seems,
Because if you will pull the problem aside
with indecision, then that problem will eat you.
Take a decision and then see !
How history make your name live forever
There is a simple rule.
End the problem before it ends you
Erase it from the root.
So that problem never rises again "

Meaning -

There is no decision that cannot be taken, every
decision can be taken. And every single decision
you take will decide whether you will win or not ?
Because people who pull the problem with
indecision, will never be able to succeed, they
won't be able to move in the right direction. They
will remain entangled only in their own confusion.
And they obstruct their own path.

That is why decisions should be taken no matter
how hard it looks because there is no such decision
which is impossible every decision is possible it's
just hard to take that decision at that moment but
that moment will define your victory, cause that
moment will determine whether you will be able to
face the situations fearlessly or will you get
defeated with the fear of the unknown.

Many people just keep thinking about making
decisions. But they get so soaked up in their
thoughts about what might be the consequences of
their decision, their thoughts become so weak that
they won't even dare to speak about their decisions
and

" then they would loose their own identity,
in the fear of losing their mask. "

And that's why we should not make our thinking
so weak that it weakens and effects us so much
that we will never be able to do anything in life.
Decide and then see how destiny will also support
you, when you stop being afraid and it will help
you reach your goals that you dream off, because
there is a simple rule, before the decision-making

dilemma and your own thinking consumes you before this fear eats you. It is better that you take a decision and face that decision firmly and put an end to that problem. Before your problems ends you, you will have to end them !

#33

Acharya Chanakya said that -

" If you need help,
then you will have to create that help for yourself "

Meaning -

It is not wrong to ask for help from people but we should become self-sufficient. We should not depend on anyone else. If we have to solve our problems completely, then we will have to be our own helpers and we will have to solve our problems on our own.

Otherwise, if we will just keep waiting for someone to help us then it is possible that we may never be able to solve that problem and we may even get entangled more in it, there is a possibility that we may get entangled in it in such a way that we may never be able to come out of it. That's why you should learn to help yourself and should not depend on someone for help or a favour.

Just like Ekalavya, a student should do his own studies, even when he gets no support or help from anyone.

Many times such problems arise in our life when our teachers are not around us, to clear our doubts, to help us. Then we will have to become like Ekalavya ourselves, then we will need to solve our own problems completely on our own without having any teachers or assistants because then you will need to be your own guru, in order to achieve the aimed.

There are many students who cannot afford tuition due to economic reasons, for them instead of getting drowned in the darkness of despair, it is better for them to be their own teachers themselves, by studying from what they have, with all their hard work, dedication and perseverance, with having faith in themselves, they will be able to achieve the needed.

You should study with your entire concentration, one needs to be truthful to oneself and get seriously dedicated in order to achieve his goal, just like Eklavya did.

Eklavya did not had a teacher. He learned archery only by practice, he made an idol of his guru infront of which he used to practice consistently, his desire to learn was so powerful that he was more proficient than Arjuna in that discipline. Arjuna had the best teacher all along to guide him through and to teach him about archery, but Ekalavya only had an idol made of that teacher which was incapable in pointing out his mistakes, but then what made him so special ?

His true desire for knowledge, his determination to achieve his desires gave him what he actually wanted, and for this reason, because of his truthfulness everyone respects him.

Because he was able to achieve what most of other students couldn't even when they got helped and were taught about this knowledge.

In exactly the same way. Every student should study on their own, by working on their abilities, by trusting themselves and by believing in themselves, even if they don't have all the resources, all the money or the books,

but these efforts must be made because these efforts only will make you different from others and will give you the courage to fight all the odds and to acquire and achieve what you are destined to achieve.

#34

Acharya Chanakya said that -

" The Greatest force is in your heart.
If this force is not weakened,
you will surely get success. "

Meaning -

Our greatest courage, our greatest strength lies in our self as our self-confidence. If we never allow ourselves to lose our faith in our abilities, then nothing can stop us from being successful.

Faith has the power to shake the thickest rock.

It is this faith that gives us courage. It is this faith that shows us the right path of life. It is this faith that teaches us that even if one falls down he should gather his courage and should rise again. And it is this faith only that makes people strong. Believe not in anyone but in yourself !

Such a belief will generates such an energy which will also encourage others to do something big, to do something good and to increase the existence of good. These incentives are as important as much as the oil is required to ignite the fire, Because the more lamps get lit, the more courage will be spread to ignite more lamps, and then that time will not be far away, when the number of knowledgeable people in the world will increase.

#35

Acharya Chanakya said that -

" If you get focused and take control over your body as well as your mind, so even an ordinary body will be able do extraordinary things. No matter how much suffering you bear. What if your mind just doesn't accepts that pain ? There are details of many such heroes in history. Whose head was severed from the torso. But they kept fighting.

They kept fighting till the last drop of their blood.
Make those warriors proud !
Tell them that you have now taken their
responsibility. "

Meaning -

It is the mind that distracts us, which is the root
cause of distraction but we can control it, only if
we want to, only if our determination to succeed,
to win is high enough to focus on the bigger
picture than being stubborn at the time and making
decisions aimlessly.

This predator, our mind preys on itself, but what if
we can reverse it, what if we can control it, in a
way to make it move in the right direction,
to make it follow the right path we want it to
follow ? It is our mind itself who sows the seeds of
doubt, If it stops sowing seeds of doubt, then trees
of despair and pain will never grow, that is if we
are able to take control, back from our mind, if we
are able to control those emotions which will no
longer hold us back, if we take the charge of our
destiny in our own hands, only then this mind will
not be able to shake us from our decisions, it will
not be able to push us into the deep gulf of doubt.
But this will not be very easy because doubts come
in everyone's mind and doubts are sometimes very
important too.
Because of them, we make our plans so good, from
the safety point of view and so properly that there
is no possibility of our plan getting failed.

But these doubts are often unreasonable and useless also.

In that case, we will have to make our mind firm by not giving in to doubt, in such a way that no idea should be able to overturn our decision and will not be able to make us stop from moving in the right direction.

'Yes', it is difficult, but not impossible.

You can control your mind only if you determined enough to do whatever it takes to stop it from being distracted and make it focus on the things which matters to you the most.

And so for the students, it is a very valuable thing to understand that they should control their mind because controlling the mind is half battle won in itself.

Because it is the mind that distracts us.

And does not let us follow our right path. Sowing the seeds of doubt, it keeps causing problems.

That is why Acharya Chanakya gave an example of those great people and told how they had so much perseverance and love for their country.

That they did not leave the truth and good !

They became immortal for the truth. In exactly the same way, every student should also Learn to control their mind by being their teachers themselves.

And then by using the knowledge one gains, one will be able to educate others.

And in this way, the flame of this knowledge will always keep burning.

#36

Acharya Chanakya said that -

" Before any important task,
close your eyes and think about your plans how
you have planned them,
how exactly will they take place,
think about all the possible circumstances/
situations that might occur, because it is beneficial
To see oneself in the dream between those
situations, Before events occur.
To live in those events in a dream.
This is also a type of preparation. "

Meaning -

Close your eyes, once in your mind, imagine your
plan, see it, feel it in the way it is going to happen
in the real life.

You can also think about the crises that may be
present at that moment hindering your plan, think
and let it flow, let every possibility hit you, let that
moment happen in every possible way, even before
it happens, don't miss a thought, a chance, look at
every aspect, just think,

Close your eyes before the war, be in the war
before it even happens so that when it does happen
you would be ready with every possible way to
play your victory again.

Because when you start looking at the situation as
if you are being a part of it in every aspect
performing different roles in your mind playing

every character you could only then you will be able to see those hidden perspectives which you might not even consider, 'being you' with your eyes open.

Be in it as if it is real, feel every part of the plan, every step you are going to take, think, just think, what if something goes wrong, what are the possible decisions or steps you will take to fix it. It will be very difficult to think about all these things during the war, because at that time you will be left with only one option to do or die, you won't think twice before taking a wrong step, because you won't have the privilege of time to think about what you are going to do,

That is why it is very important to think about everything in your dream in advance, i.e by closing your eyes, by experience the experience before it happens,

for example how will this translation of Acharya about war fit in a student's life ?

this would fit in every situation as even at war, before going for an exam or a speech one must be well prepared, or one could even end up making fool out of himself, every situation must be well planned, in order to achieve the needed, one must have options ready, keeping in mind the worse that could happened, in this way even if it does happen you will be ready to act upon it without wasting any time or sparing any time for others to cause you more trouble.

#37

Acharya Chanakya said that -

" To a pessimistic person. Every occasion will show a difficulty. But to an optimist. There is an opportunity in every difficulty. "

Meaning -

A pessimistic person, a person who is always frustrated in every situation, he/she will only see difficulty in every situation. One such person will find disappointment in every occasion and will find hundred excuses for not working. And will never be able to succeed in the task given, but an optimistic person will be able to make his own path by fighting the difficulties, even after living in difficulties, he/she will be able to find a way out of it eventually.

That is why, using these lines said by Acharya Chanakya in a students' life, one needs to understand that one should always keep their outlook optimistic and not pessimistic, one should always think good because if we will think bad about ourselves and will consider even our strengths as our weaknesses then our capabilities will deteriorated and such a perspective will not lead us anywhere in life.

If we constantly think ourselves as weak, label ourselves as weak then we will never be able to muster the courage to do something big. So what we need to do is that even if we are weak, Think that we can change it, think about improving, working on your demerits, think about getting strong. By working on oneself, one will be able to achieve the level of success one want to only if one believes, if one has the courage to face every situation with courage without getting entangled into own thoughts and doubts.

This is to say that work can be done on ourselves, whether one is weak or strong. If you believe in yourself, look at yourself from an optimistic perspective and not from a pessimistic view. Because the whole difference is made when one sees, the whole game in their own mind. Think about it, in this way that

'Every battle you will ever play will only be played in your mind, you will have to fight your own thoughts first, your inner demons, your inner weaknesses first, before fighting the opponent.'

Control the mind, tame it and start studying.

If your mind says that it will not work according to you, don't believe it, if your needs, your motives are big enough, so big that you wish to do something for the whole world, that you want to prove yourself not because of someone but because you want to truly achieve something then your mind will not be able to deter you from your decision. Your Willpower will prevent it from being distracted, Your mind Won't be able to play with you anymore.

This game is being played on you from your own mind to prevent you from being you but you will be able to resist it and will always have a choice not to play along and to be in control, your focus cannot shift it cannot deter, your focus should be so strong that even you won't be able to influence yourself anymore and this can only happen with a true determination, only if you have a true intent to achieve something, and have the will to make it work.

#38

Acharya Chanakya said that -

" We have come alone, will go alone.
Just as you do deeds, so will you bear fruit.
Forget what has passed,
Have faith in what you are doing.
whatever happens, don't worry about it.
All you have to do is to do your duties.
The task of rewarding is in the hands of your destiny and she will reward you,
Because good deeds bring good results. "

Meaning -
We have come alone in the world, you will have to face the consequences of your actions alone be it a nice deed or a bad one, everyone will have to face their own deeds one day, if you do good you will bear good, but if you do bad, be prepared for what's going to come for you.
You need to pay attention to your present situation rather than thinking about the future and the past. Your aim, your goal should, only be on your

karma, on your work, on the thing you have to do
in life and not on the results that you will get after
the completion of task, because one such person
who only focuses on the output/results will never
be able to see the difference between good or bad
or right or wrong, you don't want to be a zombie
with a goal, you have to be a human, with
perception, with moral, with the sense of what's
right for you to do and so one must think before
every action but should not only focus on results
rather one should focus on the journey,
your aim should be so strong to encourage others
to do good as well, your aim and your motives will
give you the courage to move in the right direction,
in the direction in which you are meant to move,
and will save you from getting distracted into
meaningless things.
In the Gita, Shri Krishna had also said that do your
karma and do not desire fruit. Even in the life of a
student, all his attention should only be on his
goals. Entire focus of the student should be only
on his goals and nothing else.
Many times it happens that different types of crises
arise in a students' lives, which they do not
understand how they will be able to come out of
those things. They don't see the rays of the sun to
show them the way. In such a situation a student
will have to be strong. One has to focus on his
goal, which is very difficult, but not impossible,
even while struggling with his troubles and
problems, one will have to be focused so much that
one doesn't gets distracted from his work and will

be able to see the bigger picture, even above himself/ herself.

In this (Kali-yuga) Modern world, there will be many students in the country of India, who will not have the convenience of many things, but still will all those students give up ? No ! They will face their challenges, fight with them and move on.

You will only achieve what you want to only if you will do something about it, only desires won't work, to get a desired output one needs to pay more attention to what one have and not on what one doesn't have.

By using all those things properly which we already have, by focusing and putting attention and your mind into your studies you will be able to become the better you and eventually you will be able to help others too, because

Taking is not the only purpose of human life, helping others and making everyone aware and spreading the knowledge is also very important, in order for a species to survive and grow one must be knowledgeable and aware of what's going on, otherwise the absence of knowledge and this cluelessness may bring chaos.

#39

Acharya Chanakya said that -

" Negative thinking is bad.
It is a type of infectious disease.

Which spreads a pessimistic outlook around
everyone. It should be avoided.
One should think positively.
I want positive thinking the most.
Even if the plan seems imaginable,
believe it and make it come true.
Dreamed about it before every major task
and then make it happen in reality,
Mere will, This is the basic mantra
behind every success.
Make a wish then Strongly desire it
and then get ready to fulfil it at any cost,
You will always get victory. "

Meaning -

What is a contagious disease ? An infectious
disease which spreads very quickly. Such a disease
should be eradicated from the root, it should be
eradicated in such a way that it will never disturb
the human race again, in exactly the same way,
negativity is a contagious disease in the life of any
student. A thought that always keeps the person
afraid that if he loses, he will not be able to do
anything, he might not be able to stand up again,
face himself again.

Such thoughts are the most dangerous ones, even
more dangerous than the poison itself, because
such kind of thinking makes one incapable of
anything, even the things he/she could do before
he/she won't be able to do that now because they
think bad about themselves, when people lose hope
and feel neglected, unworthy, not capable then

they stop working and eventually take such paths which will only lead them to their destruction. Brain feeds on these thoughts and produces the outcomes accordingly and so one must set himself/herself free from such thinking,
you can think of this in this way that this is the kind of thinking that makes a human hollow from inside, from within, in the exact same way just like when the termites eat the wood and makes it hollow, in such a way that the wood would be drained out from it's meaning of existence and then that wood becomes so empty and useless that even in the trash, it has no work.

That is why, realising our mistakes is important, that our thinking was wrong and now the time has come to change that thinking. It is time that we accept that whatever our thinking has been till now, but from now on and we will keep an optimistic view about life, That from today we will always think well of ourselves.

Because a positive thought gives us that courage, it gives passion, to fulfil the assigned task, to achieve our goals, to reach the designated place where we are meant to be.

Acharya Chanakya also explains to us that even if the plan seems imaginable, Even then we should trust it so that we can fulfil it, Because if you will not even believe in the imagination of your plan, then forget about completing it you even won't be able to focus or concentrate.

and so you must have faith in your plans. Only then will you be able to give concrete shape to those plans.

And how exactly will this happen ? With your strong will, With the help of your confidence in yourselves and with your positive thinking. These three things will give you such a force that your attention will never deviate from your goal, because even if it does you will be the one reminding yourself about the importance of the task, that why it must be completed, why is it important to you, your needs will not let your thoughts wander in the wrong direction and will always make you to focus on the right path, because you won't have the luxury of choice of letting your thoughts wander in the wrong direction because your aim, your goal by then will become your priority.

#40

Acharya Chanakya said that -

" Courage is not in being afraid,
It is in your facing fears. "

Meaning -
Courage is in this thing that we face our fears. Do not run away from them, but be ready to fight your enemy against your fears. Be prepared for this that at some point in life you will have to face your fears. You will have to overcome your fear and win. For that, you will have to be courageous and will have to believe in yourself and make yourself

so capable that even your fear would get know that you won't get afraid now, you won't compromise, you won't kneel, from now on you will take charge of your own life, no matter how hard it is, but your will try and will defeat your worst enemy your own fear, your confidence your courage should from now on speak on your behalf and from this moment you won't be afraid because you won't allow yourself to be.

To achieve victory, first of all we should know our weaknesses ! Because if we do not know our weaknesses then we will not be able to overcome them. We can only be frightened as long as we are afraid of this fear. But what if we stop being afraid of this fear ? But how is this possible ?

This is possible in such a way that we have to work on our shortcomings, that is, fear can only frighten us, only when it knows our weaknesses, when it knows how to use those weaknesses to pressurise us, to intimidate us, but what if we make our weaknesses our strength ? What If we work on those weaknesses and eliminate those weaknesses ? and convert them into something that this fear won't expect us to, we have that power, that choice to make things right, to work on ourselves, to improve ourselves so why not use this quality to eliminate our bad habits, our weaknesses and start improvising and accepting, The existence of fear will disappear on its own when we will start to change ourselves, when we will improve, accept, familiarise and overcome the hurdles which kept stopping us from moving on, facing the problems and dealing with them,

standing against the opponent looking him in the eyes , without accepting this fear as your master and being in charge yourself is they key,
If you bow to your fear, then it will always be there to haunt you, and will keep you imprisoned but if you accept it's existence and start facing it with courage then it won't be able to bother you again because then there will be nothing left to fear from, your fear will fade away, he will be treated in the same way he used to treat you, and will lose and will get diminished.

#41

Acharya Chanakya said that -

" When a person has to move forward,
So first he sets his goal And when that person
moves towards the goal, Sets out on the road
So the passage he takes that passage teaches him.
That ride makes him who he is
and so this experience is his real capital.
The goal is reached by walking on the path
and the object to be attained
is only an indicative achievement.
The real achievement is the learning on the way ! "

Meaning -
The real achievement of any person
is not determined by the result or goal he/she
achieves but it is determined by the learning he

gets on the way. The experiences he gets along the way. For example, suppose there is a student who has secured first place in his class. And he has got a gold medal.

So the gold medal that student has got is just an symbolic achievement. This is to say that the gold medal simply shows that he has passed a phase of his life in a very good way. But the actual achievement is not that medal.

But what he has learned in that year is the real achievement of that student. Through education, what he has learned, the things he read, the manner in which he has learned to write, speak, the manner in which his personality and character has improved is the real achievement of that student. And that same achievement, Will really help that student to move forward in his life. Because even if that student got the gold medal, still that medal won't be able to save him from the serious obstacles which might come in his way, from the challenges which he/she will face in the future, the only thing which can save him is his own mind which has developed and improved with the help of the knowledge which he has gained in that year. That is why the real achievement is not what we consider as the real achievement. That is, the real achievement is not a medal or any award. His knowledge is his real achievement ! The real achievement is the capital of experience that he has collected that year, in which he has received the gold medal, those experiences , those challenges that he has faced till now, all that knowledge will guide his way in the future.

#42

Acharya Chanakya said that -

" Control your thoughts.
Because they will become your voice.
Keep your voice under control.
Because it will become your actions.
Control your actions.
Because they will become your habits.
Control your habits.
Because they will build your character.
And control your character.
Because it will make your fortune. "

Meaning -

Acharya Chanakya is trying to explain us in these above lines that
How we have to make our fortune ?
That is, how do we have to lead our future life,
But on what will it depend ?
It will depend on a lot of things.
First of all, for example firstly a student should learn to control his/her thoughts
Just as optimistic thoughts encourage a person, it gives courage.
And pessimistic thoughts break a person's morale.
These thoughts are also very important because these thoughts get reflected in a person's words when he/she speaks, these thoughts can clearly be seen in one's speech,

That is why it is very important for any student to control his/her thoughts.

Because if one is able to control his thoughts, by simply doing this he/she will also be able to control his words, his voice what he/she speaks, His words will become tamed. For example, in the words of a student who has been taught well, he will not even have to prove anything, the way in which he speaks will clearly show and reflect that weather he has been taught well or not,

for example he will not use dirty words in his speech but some students use dirty words, those words are not merely just words but they depict their thinking, their thoughts, That is why one should keep his thoughts and speech in control, because whatever we will think we will speak according to that, and whatever we will speak our behaviour will get moulded according to that and so our behaviour should be for public welfare and not for dirty things,

Because If we have got this life, then we should use it properly. For the good of all, one should not to promote dirty thoughts. And when a student can subdue his deeds. So his habits will also improve on their own.

That is, if a student has to get first place in his class, then for that he has to subdue his actions every day. One habit has to be formed that he will have to study from all his heart and with full commitment and concentration, Only then will he be able to achieve the position he wants to.

#43

Acharya Chanakya said that -

" No person is extraordinary. But when an ordinary person gets caught in extraordinary circumstances. So while solving them That ordinary person also looks extraordinary. This is the quality of a true king. "

Meaning -

No person is extraordinary, but when he is caught in such situations, in which either he will win everything or won't even be left with anything in such a situation he can either fight with the courage or run away taking shame, His character will be tested at that time. His will power is being tested at that time, It is a test whose results will determine that will he be able to dare and become someone important or will he lose himself forever in the sea of defeat.

For example, there will come a time in a student's life in which he too will have to face this situation which will test his strength by giving him the option either to fight or to flight, that moment will be the most crucial moment in his life and will determine who he will become in future, his character will evolve from that single decision, that he will take at that moment, he will have a choice to that either he can live in the present by facing the situations or he can disappear in the past and live in this misery forever by regretting the decision he made and this decision will truly test his knowledge, either he wins by using this true power of knowledge or gets defeated by getting entangled in the complications of his own thoughts, this choice will test him, At such a time, if he makes the right choice then he will definitely succeed in his life. But if he does not make the right choice, he will lose himself in his own eyes. And then he might not get a chance to come back again, the second chance which everyone awaits but hardly anyone gets it because by that time it gets too late,

That is why it is very important to make the right choice at the right time. And for that we will have to decide everything with patience in every situation.

#44

Acharya Chanakya said that -

" Who never committed any error in his life.
What did he learn from his life ? "

Meaning -

Making an error is not wrong, making a mistake is not wrong, Because we get to learn only through errors, but it is also not right that we kept doing the same mistakes again and again all our life,

in a student's life making mistakes not deliberately but by chance is a good medium of getting experience, to learn such a lesson, which he will cherish and which will remind him not to do the same mistakes again and those mistakes will help him make a solid foundation of a better life, but this does not means that they should make countless errors just to learn and remember, also one must always remember not to get associated in such task which are not good or are not planned with a good intension, Acharya Chanakya has used the word mistake in the sense to convey that one must not fear from encountering experiences or should not be afraid to experience because every mistake we do, it makes us a better person, it molds us, corrects us gives us the courage to improve and try again, those experiences are priceless and if we are willing to learn then even those mistakes will be fruitful for us because we will learn from them, those mistakes will teach us, But we should also remember this as well That it is also not necessary that we make all the mistakes ourselves. We can also learn from the mistakes of others. You can also learn by watching others. This will save time and one will be able to correct his mistakes before even they could occur, that is why one must learn from the previous mistakes of oneself and of other people but also one should not be scared of new experiences of doing mistakes , because this fear won't let you do anything, it wont let you experience or try new things. And our effort should be that we learn more from the mistakes of others. So that there are fewer obstacles in our route, for example is you know a student is not able to achieve his desired goal, is

not able to score well then you can ask such a
student what was the reason behind his failure ?
was he not concentrating well enough, did he gave
proper to time to his studies ? or was he pre-
occupied by some problems ? if that students says
that he did not study well do to so and so reason,
then one can learn from his mistakes and one
should try not to repeat those mistakes in order to
be successful, always remember one should know
that perfection also takes time, practice and
courage of accepting the mistakes one has done,
there is nothing wrong in acceptance, we need to
accept and improvise because that is the real key to
the path of success.

#45

Acharya Chanakya said that -

" Who is super intelligent ? Someone more
intelligent than the commoners, in a crisis
intelligence will not matter, only those will survive
who will have the ability to adaptability, who will
adapt according to the circumstances "

Meaning -
highly intelligent people, less intelligent people,
using new words for intelligence will only increase
our dictionary. No one will be saved from crisis.
Only those will be able to survive the crisis who
will have the ability to adapt, to change

themselves, Will have the ability to convert oneself, to put oneself in tune with the circumstances, Only he will be able to escape from the crisis.

Along with the questions, destiny does write down their answers. They are in front of us, only we are not willing to find them. We don't just have to give up, to find that answer you will have to continuously make efforts and will have to continue the journey,

It is possible that any student once in his lifetime may get trapped in such a crisis which he did not expected to be in and being in an unexpected situation it is possible that he may not see a way out of it, what to do then, in such a situation ?

for example if students are told that they will have a surprise test, they won't be able to quite it, because of being present in the class at that time, but they will have a chance to adapt to have the courage and ask the teacher to give them the time to revise or study, in this way they will eventually pass the test but if they kept talking and fighting against the teacher then that teacher may never get convinced even to give them the time they need for revision, one must learn to blend in, to mix up and to adapt, in order to survive one must do so.

and then it is better that they start studying in all time that is left with them. Because one needs to blend according to the circumstances, complying with the ability to adapt. Because when we know that we will not be able to change our circumstances, then the solution to escape that situation will already means defeat, in order to win you will have to adapt, without letting your ego hinder your decision, because ego will lead you nowhere it will just destroy you and will only become a stone in your path which will be always there to make you stop, to make sure that you don't move forward, whereases adaptation, the path to change, survival instinct will require for you to be bold, to have the courage to say what's needed to be said or you wont get the second chance and above of all this, <u>change will demand your ego to be played with, it will test you in ways you would have never thought to be possible</u>, one must be ready to accept whatever life throws at you, because your goal is not just to win a war but it is also to survive it.

#46

Acharya Chanakya said that -

" A true hero
will not lead by force or deceit
But will lead his teammates
by setting an example. "

Meaning -
If we need cooperation,
Even if we get the help with force or deceit, it will definitely reduce it's impact in the future, for example one may compromise and cooperate for the fear you will force but they will always plan to

betray to stand against you which is right in a way, that is human nature to stand against the bad ones, life is not about ruling, it is more about leading, showing them the right way,
one may surrender to circumstances but loyalty exceeds even faith and loyalty comes from trust, by being on the right side.
That is why a true hero should set his intellect and lead an example by showing everyone the right path to be in, by walking at that path himself, one must not aim to dictate, to rule, but one must try to take everyone with him and to win everyone's heart.
Because goodness is in taking everyone along, divide and rule may work for sometime but it wont let people breathe, neither your true self would allow you such an act, one must gain the confidence of the people he want by his side not by force or deceit, but by their will,
because if you will get the support of the people by their wish, by their will, then the importance of that cooperation will increases further and eventually you will gain their loyalty, which is far more important in order to lead than anything else.

#47

Acharya Chanakya said that -

" Time's beating heart is the only possibility. "

Meaning -

The possibility is hidden in time itself.

Time is the key !

In ancient times, in the time of kings. There were problems in the court and the ministers of the kings and if their principal advisors were not able to solve those problems, then they would used to asked the king for some time, they used to take time to think, to act, to understand the problem, 'yes', only king had the right to decide the fate of the person that whether he/she is guilty or not but even they were wise enough to wait, not to take any decision without advise,

because

" time is a luxury not everyone can afford but the people who can, definitely have an advantage over the others ",

because one can reach the right solution when one thinks well enough about the problem taking all the time which is needed to reach the required conclusion,

that is why it is very important for any person, for a human being to understand the fact that if you are unable to find the best solution for your problem then you must take your time, to understand that problem well enough in order to react or to find the best way out of it .

Have patience, time has all the power,

it can heal as well as destroy,

take your time and you will find your way out !

#48

Acharya Chanakya said that -

" The greatest weapon is man's intelligence and his conscience. A wise warrior with his wisdom tact and prudence can help him get victory in any war, then it won't matter how odd the circumstances will be at that time "

Meaning -

The greatest weapon for any person is his own wisdom tact. Because the blow from the lining of the intellect never goes empty.
The problems we go through everyday,
They too come from someone's intellect.
for example - some people create their own problems because of their own stupidity, there is a saying:
" That if the axe did not fall on the foot, then he went to the axe and hit his foot on it knowingly. "
There are many people in the same way who are the cause of their own problems.
Intellect is the key, it has the power which can solve or create the biggest problems ever, it depends on how you use the intellect you have. Wisdom is such a weapon from which any thought that comes out it is so powerful that, just like a arrow that thought if used wisely, can become harmful or can even heal just like a medicine, it will totally depends on the will and intent of that

person, what he/she is willing to do with such a knowledge,

That is why intelligence should not be underestimated.

for example if there is a student who wants to clear a certain entrance exam but he/she doesn't have the right books or the right material to study from, that is he/she may not have the right weapon, But as long as he/she has his intelligence, no one can beat him/her.

Yes, he may not be able to figure out every question but at least he can try, as long as he is not willing to give up, there will always be a chance for him to win, let's say he is unable to purchase some books, even if he can't buy he can always look up the free versions of those books on the internet, this is to say that as long as he is willing to try he will eventually find a way, he can ask his friends, for help to explain him the concepts he is unable to understand, can always borrow books from library, and there are many other countless ways, if one uses his intelligence, If you want to succeed in life or in any other situation there is a simple rule, that you must not give up !

You will have to face your problems with the utter most courage and confidence,

Because one who will be scared to see the problem itself, will eventually run away. He will never see success in his life.

If you really want to win then you must face the problem and you will see that facing your problems with courage will ultimately pave your path for winning.

#49

Acharya Chanakya said that -

" When you will have more than one choice,
and it will be hard to take any decision,
so at that time one must concentrate with his full
attention and should listen to the signs of his
conscience, because the signs of the conscience are
never wrong. "

Meaning -
When you are entangled in the choice of many
options and don't know in which direction to go,
which path to take then what should one do at that
time ? when in such a distress, calm yours self
down, focus your attention and think because when
we calmly make selections, only then do those
selections come out right.
For example if a student is not able to decide his
career or goal in his life, that is what is the right
path for him ? then one should surely take time to
think but one should not get entangled in thinking
only because taking action is also as much as
important as thinking is, if the right time of
making decision passes away then, there is a
possibility that you may never get a second chance
and so one must clam his mind and then try to
concentrate and then with the help of your own
questions, you will have to find out your best
options to choose from, example in this case
finding and discovering self in order to know

oneself better one should find his/her interests and then choose his/her career accordingly, because the right road taken is the first step to success, and your first step will eventually lead your way to your success. For such a person who is not able to find the purpose, the right career path, one can ask himself/herself these questions -

- first question - What is it or what subject is it which makes me loose time ? while studying or doing such thing i loose the count of time, there has to be something which grabs your attention in such a way that you not only loose the track of time but also become unaware of your surroundings while doing so, your attention automatically is focused on that task and it doesn't even deviate, this is the subject which you don't have to force study, " <u>it's not compelled on you but it compels you</u> ", there has to be something which you don't study only from your mind but also from your heart, find it !

- second question - Which career is meant for me ? is it practical ? or do i have other options ? Which goal/path would take me to my success ? Keeping one's circumstances and economic conditions in mind, one will have to decide this.

- Third question - Has this been my goal since childhood ? Is this what I wanted to be from the start or is it that it has changed ? if deviated then you might be thinking practically, taking decisions practically is the only option for some people, it depends from situation to situation but if it hasn't been deviated that is if your dream and your goal from your childhood has been one and you still wish to do it, then you must go for it and should be able to convince your family since you are so passionate about it, you will be able to convince them, Because we also need to understand that life is very short; max to max what ? 100 years for a healthy living person.

He has to become something in these 100 years, Something has to be done. A goal has to be attained, a goal that he/she is born to achieve.

A true objective will be one in which when one climbs the ladder of success, then his duty should be to help others achieve their goals to help the human race and this will make him immortal, who is immortal, a person who can live forever right ? such a person who will help the human race will become immortal as every single person will keep him alive in their memories,

but still someone will always ask why see such big dream ? if not everyone will be able to achieve it ? but i say, some will and that's what matters and maybe you will be able to achieve this level of success too, who know what your destiny await maybe you are just a step away.

The same goes for being remembered and being immortal if you will ask that is it possible, can it ever happen ? The answer is "yes", When the goal is too big and is in public welfare.

It depends on the student's thinking what he/she wants to become. But whatever decision you make, do remember this That when we take something from the world as we learn, it becomes our duty to give something to the same world !

Whether it is to share your knowledge, to distribute wealth or to help anyone, because in the end it's not just about taking everything we can, but one must also learn to give to this world, a better living, a better place and a better future.

#50

Acharya Chanakya said that -

" No problem can defeat hope.
No night can stand in front of the sun rise. "

Meaning -

There is no problem on which victory cannot be achieved. The solution to each problem arises with the same problem, the day the problem arises on its own. That is why one should never give up hope. It should never be forgotten that there is always a solution to every problem. The solution is there it's just that we are not able to find it out yet, Therefore, one should wait and then should carefully find a solution for that problem. Acharya has given a very good example here, regarding sun and night, that there is no such night which can stop the sun from rising. The sun rises and stays there. It stays in front of you. Solutions also remain the same way, they come out in the same manner. We should never stop trying, to find

solutions to our problems one should keep
searching till that problem is solved.
It is possible that it will take us very long to find
the perfect solution that we need but we will only
find it if we are willing not to give up.
But then
" What's that problem ?
Which gets resolved very quickly,
And what is that solution ?
which gets found by itself without trying "

—————————————

" Guru Brahma
Gurur Vishnu
Guru Devo Maheshwaraha
Guru Saakshat Para Brahma
Tasmai Sree Gurave Namaha "

Meaning -

Guru is verily the representative of Brahma,
Vishnu and Shiva. He creates, sustains
knowledge and destroys the weeds of
ignorance. I salute such a Guru.

YouTube channel -   IT'S SIMPLE - Priyanka
Instagram id -   @itssimplepriyanka
Facebook page -   @itssimplepriyanka
Twitter -   @itssimplepri

Made in the USA
Monee, IL
13 June 2022

97937645R00059